Dream Killers

ALMA THOMAS

P.O. Box 841
Tobyhanna, PA 18466
(973) 348-5067
sspublishingcompany@gmail.com
www.sharsheypublishingcompany.com

Copyright © 2016 Alma Thomas
ISBN: 13: 978-0-9972668-7-0
ISBN: 10: 0-9972668-7-2
Publisher: Shar- Shey Publishing Company LLC
Book Cover Designed by: Dynasty's Visionary Designs
Edited by: Tricia Drammeh

All rights reserved. No part of this book may be reproduced or transmitted in any form or by any means, electronic or mechanical, including photocopying, recording, or by any information storage and retrieval system, without permission in writing from the copyright owner. This book was printed in the United States of America.

DEDICATION

This book is dedicated to Tysean Marvis Laurence Thomas, my beloved son who left his earthly home to move to his heavenly home. Continue to sleep in peace, baby, until that great getting up morning in the sky.

April 17, 1990- February 13, 2009

Chapter One

Are You A Dreamer Or A Visionary?

And it shall come to pass that I will pour my spirit out on all flesh, and your sons and daughters shall prophesy and your old men shall see visions. (Acts 2:17)

As children, we are all dreamers. We spend countless hours dreaming about what we are going to be when we grow up, or what type of house we will live in. As children, we were not afraid to dream big; no dream was too big. We would spend countless hours dreaming about being a famous ballerina and we would see visions of us on the big stage dancing *Swan Lake*, or we would picture us making the big shot at the all-star game. All of us as children shared a common characteristic—we were all dreamers, but somewhere along this journey called life we stopped dreaming.

We had vivid imaginations, but as time went on some of us stopped dreaming and allowed our dreams to slowly die.

We are taught at an early age that it is not good to be a dreamer, but we should go to school and obtain an education and get a good job.

"We are not encouraged as children to be entrepreneurs or risk takers, we are told that as adults we have to responsible and dependable and responsible adults do not chase dreams." ~ Robert Sharma.

Dreamers are often mocked as being impractical and having their heads in the clouds, but that is not true because their creativity and innovations typically lead to a better way of life for us all. Therefore, the first thing that a dreamer must possess is a dream.

Do you believe deep in your heart that God is calling you to something greater? Do you often visualize God using you to impact the lives of others?

DREAM KILLERS

There is a difference between the dreams that you dream at night while you are sleeping and the dreams that determine your purpose in life. The dreams that you dream at night are a series of thoughts, images, and sensations that occur in a person's mind during sleep. The dream that determines your purpose in life is a strong desire, goal, or purpose.

Just for a moment, go back to the place in your life when being a dreamer was considered cool. Close your eyes and imagine that you are living your dream life. Describe what your life would look like if there were no limitations on money, time, or resources. Just imagine all your dreams coming true. It would be like a fairy tale that, no matter what circumstances or situations you went through in life, in the end you will marry your prince charming and live happily ever after.

A dream is a mental picture that you paint in your mind. A dreamer can visualize in their minds life as it should be, not as it is now. Vision is where your dreams and desires and your need to be in the future meet. For your dreams to be manifested in your life, you must have clear-cut goals and aspirations. One of my favorite quotes is: "If your mind can conceive it and your heart can believe it then you can achieve it." It is a mind thing - all dreams that start in your mind and that are fueled by your passions will eventually be manifested. Helen Keller who was physically blind said, "The only thing worse than being blind is having sight but no vision."

Helen Keller, who was blind and could not see out of her natural eyes, believed that even worse than not having the sense of sight, is not having a sense of direction or purpose for your life. To achieve anything in your life you should be able to picture it for yourself. You will never rise above the image that you have of yourself. You will never accomplish anything until you can envision yourself accomplishing it.

Ever since I was a little girl, I loved to read. As a matter of fact, it was one of my escape mechanisms. I would read and imagine that whatever characters in the book that I chose, I was them rather than me. I always wanted to be a writer so I could portray characters living the life that I always wanted.

Over the years, I accumulated countless notebooks of partially written books, poetry, and plays. Other times, I experienced writer's block and could not write a word.

All my life, my teacher told me that I was a good writer and throughout the years I have had many stories to tell. But I allowed rejection, fear, and lack of finances to discourage me and began to lose the desire to even write. I slowly found myself in the sea of wannabees. I want to be this or I want to be that - always wanting, but never achieving.

This book was birthed out of an article that I was asked to write for a magazine and as I was thinking about what I was going to write about, God whispered, 'Dream Killers.' I answered, 'what are you trying to tell me God?' And he answered, 'you allowed people and things to kill your dreams.'

The book that I was writing for five years from the waiting room to the recovery room was almost finished. I just had a few more chapters to write, but I just could not finish the last chapter and God said, 'this is not just another case of a book that you start and never finish.

This time it is much deeper than that. The reason why you cannot complete the book is because you are not in the recovery room yet, but you are still in the delivery room because somewhere along the line, something tried to kill your dreams.'

Over the years, I have read many inspirational and motivational books, but still had not achieved total deliverance. As I was writing this book, I felt emotional chains falling off and deliverance taking place in my areas of my life that were important to me achieving my purpose in life. I understood that in the spiritual realm a change was taking place in my life. I began to start to plan my book signing event and my first conference, *The Dream Killers Dare to Dream Again Conference*. The words for the book began to flow as steadily as the tears out of my eyes. In two weeks, the first draft was written and I finally saw myself as a published author. There was finally a transition in my life from dreamer to visionary. Vision means mental sight, dreams, or revelations.

Vision is the ability to see your dreams come to fruition in your mind. Vision is God's definition for your life. It is a mental blueprint of our dreams, visions, and aspirations and the action plans that you need to achieve them. Vision is the bridge that allows you to travel from your past into your future. Vision is the ability to see what others think is impossible.

There are people who sit in the garbage cans of life, smelling and stinky and allowing people to continue to throw garbage on them, always saying that they want better, but never making plans to get out of the garbage can. All they had to do was get out of the can. There were so many times in my life when I desired more, but refused to climb out of the can. There have been so many times in life when I was pregnant with purpose, but I miscarried the baby. Giving birth is a process, but you will never give birth to anything until you conceive and you will never carry full term if you don't protect your fetus from negative influence.

To birth your dream, you must first have a dream and then you must nurture it until it's born. Close your eyes one more time. What do you see for your life? With your eyes, closed, you should see more than what you see with them open.

Let's look at the lives of two young women born and raised with the same socioeconomic backgrounds and same dysfunctional family, but their lives took very different turns.
They are both the products of a single parent home and there was no father in the picture. They attended the same schools and their mothers both had the same welfare mentality, but one becomes a stripper and the other a doctor. What was the difference?

What made the difference in the paths that these two young ladies took in life?

The difference was their mindsets. One decided that she was not going to allow her past to dictate her future. She was determined that she would break the generational curse that was on her family and the spirit of poverty. She studied hard in school, graduated valedictorian, went to college on a full scholarship, and eventually graduated from medical school. The other young girl fell victim to her circumstances and believed that she was destined to repeat the past of her mother, and she choose to start cutting school and partying. She eventually had a baby out of wedlock and dropped out of school, and with no vocational skills, she started stripping to support her family.

Another difference is that one saw the obvious reality of her current situation and circumstances, and she became dismayed and discouraged. The other had a dream that turned into a vision, and she understood that your past doesn't have to dictate your future.

Dreamers are people who view life with expectancy, hope, and limitless opportunities. It is all in your perspective and how you view the situation. The main difference between people that live their dreams, and those that die with their dreams within them, is perspective. A dreamer with vision is willing to explore the odds and take chances.

Are you a dreamer or a visionary? Visionaries are a rare breed because many people are not willing to take a chance. There are risks that you must undertake to be a visionary. Visionaries will often fail many times before they succeed. Denis Waitley, a motivational speaker, said:

> *"Failure should be our teacher, not our undertaker. Failure is delay, not defeat. It is a temporary detour, not a dead end. Failure is something we can avoid only by saying nothing, doing nothing, and being nothing."*

To turn a dream into a reality, there must be a vision. In life, not all dreamers are visionaries, but all visionaries are dreamers.

Do not despise small beginnings for who hath despised the day of small things? for they shall rejoice, and shall see the plummet in the hand of Zerubbabel with those seven; they are the eyes of the LORD, which run to and fro through the whole earth. (Zechariah 4:10)

Every idea starts small. It develops in someone's mind, matures into a vision, and eventually manifests as a reality. The world is full of dreamers. They come a dime a dozen. It really doesn't cost you anything to dream, but a vision comes with a cost. There will be many times as you go from dreamer to visionary that you will want to give up. You will question if it is worth it. Many times, you must remind yourself how bad you really want it.

We like to peek into the backyards of people who are living their dream life. We see the manifestation of glory, but we do not know the intimate details of their story. We do not know the cost.

For your dreams to be revealed, they are going to cost your something. It will cost you time, money, and effort. For years, I had dreams of being a best-selling author, that I would write the books that would empower women and change their lives. But at that time, I never knew the cost. The things that I would have to go through to be able to write my story, and then getting that story out to the world, were not free. So, year after year, I sat and just dreamed about sharing my story with the world.

Dreamers make plans, but they never finish anything that they start. Visionaries on the other hand make plans that will turn their dreams into reality. The dreamer is satisfied with merely dreaming about a better life. Visionary people face the same problems everyone else faces, but rather than get paralyzed by their problems, visionaries immediately commit themselves to finding a solution.

DREAM KILLERS

"We all have dreams. But in order to make dreams come into reality, it takes an awful lot of determination, dedication, self-discipline, and effort." ~ Bill Hybels

We are all dreamers. We often sit year after year thinking of our 'if onlys'—if only I had a better job, if only I graduated from college—but never taking the steps necessary to make our dreams a reality. Toba Beta said, "visionaries build what dreamers only imagine."

It's a process. Your dreams should determine your goals and your goals should cause you to move. Action creates results. A vision demands a change in your mindset, thoughts and deeds. It takes courage to be a visionary—you cannot be a scaredy cat and a visionary at the same time. A dreamer is satisfied with the status quo; they are comfortable in their comfort zone. But a visionary is willing to try something they never tried before to get something they never had before; they are willing to step outside of their comfort zone to achieve their dreams.

Before you continue reading, it's time for you to take a long, hard look into the mirror and ask yourself these questions:

- Are you a dreamer or a visionary?
- Are you satisfied sitting on the dock of the bay, wasting time and daydreaming, or are you a visionary?
- Are you ready to take your dreams to the next level?
- Are you ready to take this trip from dreamer to visionary?

I must warn you beforehand, that it will not be an easy journey. There will be detours, delays, and road closings along the way.

In the next chapter, you will be asked to ID your dream killers. They have someone in custody and you need to positively ID the factors that killed your dreams. It is time to come face to face with your dream killers.

Chapter Two

Dream Killers

The thief cometh not, but for to steal, and to kill, and to destroy: I am come that they might have life, and that they might have it more abundantly. (John 10:10)

In John 10:10, we fathom that the thief's desire is to come, to steal, kill, and destroy. The enemy recognizes that God has a plan for your life and he is on an assignment to block, destroy, or abort God's plan. One of my favorite people in the Bible is Joseph. Joseph was a dreamer and he had a lot of haters in his life. Joseph had an anointing on his life and he had a lot of people on assignment to block, destroy, or abort. Joseph had a dream concerning his brothers. They got upset when he told them about the dream and they plotted to kill him.

They wanted to eradicate the anointing that Joseph had on his life. It was more than that multicolored coat that he received from his father, but it was what that coat represented that they wanted to destroy—the Father's anointing on his life.

Do you realize that people will hate on you because of the anointing that you have on your life? All my life I had to face hater after hater and I just could not understand why people hated on me. In the natural sense, I didn't have anything but a dollar and a dream. I was barely existing, living from paycheck to paycheck, surviving on just enough, and people that seemingly had it going on were always hating on me. So I started my own personal journey from dreamer to visionary. God began to reveal to me what was happening in my life and it wasn't me per se, but the anointing that was on my life. They saw the anointing on my life before I did, but what they did not see was all the hell that I have gone through for this anointing. The fire that was meant to burn up my destiny.

When Joseph dreamed that one day his brother would bow down to him, the enemy stepped in and tried to eradicate the dream and the dreamer. It's important to understand that the adversary will only try to massacre your dreams when you are in the process of making your daydreams into a vision. The enemy only gets stirred up when he realizes that you are more than just a dreamer. He doesn't care how much time you waste in la la land. The enemy and his kingdom are not threatened by you just dreaming about sharing your life-changing testimony with the world; it is when you stop being a wannabe, that is when you better watch out because now the enemy is after you.

The enemy was sitting on the sidelines laughing his behind off when I was just talking about all the ideas that God was placing in my spirit. The enemy and my dream killers would constantly ask me with a smirk on their faces, *how is that book coming along?*

But when I started to write this book and I felt some many chains falling off me, it was then that the devil got mad as hell at me.

So, you need to understand that you are no threat to the enemy while you are just talking about writing a book, finishing school, or starting a business—the devil is just laughing at you. But I dare you to enroll in school, get an EIN number, or start writing that book—just do something to make your dream into a reality, start to make plans to bring that dream to manifestation. The devil doesn't mind you sleeping, but it is when you wake up that you become armed and dangerous. It's when you wake up that you aggravate the devil and that is when you become a marked target for assassination.

It is when I decided that enough is enough and I was tired of living beneath my privilege that all hell broke loose in my life. I was tired of sleeping on my God-given talents and gifts, tired of begging God for a solution and God telling me that I already had all that I needed for success. It was now that the devil launched an all-out attack, when I finally started to realize my self-worth, and that it was long overdue for me to stop talking and start walking into my destiny.

The enemy came in like a flash flood and attacked my ministry, finances, relationship, and even my self-confidence. I came to realize that the enemy had strategically placed dream killers in my camp: in my family, job, and supposedly close relationships. They were designed to kill my dreams.

In Genesis 37, we find an episode out of the life of Joseph:

> *Now Israel loved Joseph more than all of his other children because he was the son of his old age and he made him a coat of many colors. And when his brethren saw their father loved him more than all his brethren they hated him and could not speak peaceably unto him. And Joseph dreamed a dream and he told his brethren and they hated him yet the more.*

And he said unto them, hear I pray you, this dream which I have dreamed. For behold we were binding sheaves in the field and, lo my sheaf arose, and stood around about and made obeisance to my sheaf. And, his brethren said to him shall thou indeed reign over us, or shall thou have dominion over us, and they hated him yet the more for his dream, and for his words. And he dreamed yet another dream, and told it his brethren and said Behold, I have dreamed a dream more and behold, the sun and the moon and the eleven stars made obeisance to me, and he told it to his father and his father rebuked him and said unto him, What is this dream that thou hast dreamed? Shall I and thy mother and thy brethren indeed come to bow down ourselves to thee to the earth? And his brethren envied him. But his father observed this saying. (Genesis 37:3-11)

In biblical times, authority in the family is ranked in age from the eldest to youngest. Per traditions, Joseph should have gladly accepted his role as servant to his older brothers because he was the baby at that time.

Sometimes in life you must go against what is considered politically correct. A real dreamer will not allow the status quo to hinder them. A dreamer is not bound by traditions. There is a passion deep inside of a dreamer that will not accept the identity that society has destined for them; there is something that is nestled deep inside of each and every one of us that decrees that we are destined for more than what we presently see our present situation is, not our destination.

You need to understand, my beloved, that where you are now is not your final resting place. People might have already given up on you and buried you. All my life I was told that I would never amount to anything.

But look at this little poor girl from Mississippi, look what God has done. I am a witness that God can take an ordinary person and do extra-ordinary things through them.

> *Verily, verily, I say unto you, He that believeth on me, the works that I do shall he do also; and greater works than these shall he do; because I go unto my Father."*
> *(John 14:12)*

I am telling you that the place where you are now is not a stopping place, but it is your launching pad; the things that you are going through at this present time is preparing you for greater purpose. God is lifting you to another level.

I hear people saying that they feel a shifting in the atmosphere and they want God to shift them. I heard Apostle JD Rucker from Junaid Ministry say on her prayer line that we don't want a shift, but we need a lifting.

So I re-searched the difference between the two and what I discovered is that I don't want to be shifted, but I aspire to be lifted a little higher.

Per Webster Dictionary, shift means to move from one place to another, especially over a small distance or a slight change in position, direction or tendency. Lift means to raise to a higher position or level. Pick up and move to a different position.

When you begin to act upon your dreams, you are no longer happy with mediocre. People can no longer control or manipulate you to stay in that same situation or circumstance that the dream finds you in. The things that used to thrill you no longer turn you on. The idea of God shifting you no longer appeals to you, but you now desire to go to higher heights and deeper depths. Your visions will always propel you into a prominent future.

Let's look at Joseph's life again. As a child, Joseph's dream of promotion was very exciting to him. He could not wait to share his good news with his friends and especially his family, but not everyone was excited about his dreams.

Joseph's family, those folks who he thought would have had his back and share in his excitement for what God was about to manifest in his life—the same ones who he thought would celebrate with him, were the same ones who ridiculed him and hated on him. Those folks that he thought would have been his cheerleaders were his biggest haters. The ones who said, 'who do you think are Mr. Big Stuff,' when they looked and saw him coming, they murmured among themselves 'here comes that dreamer again.' And they plotted together to kill him and his dreams.

Look back over your life and reflect on the people that you shared your dream with, who were your dream killers. Was it someone who you thought that you could trust with your dreams aspirations and visions? People that you believed would be happy when you announced that you were pregnant with purpose? Some of them congratulated you in front of your face, but plotted against you behind your back.

Some of them you trusted enough to allow them into your delivery room to be your midwives, but while you were under anesthesia they tried to abort your baby; they were never your friends, but they were dream killers that had been placed in your life to abort or steal your babies.

Those same people who you thought were praying for you and celebrating your pregnancy were secretly speaking death to your dreams and visions.

One hard pill to swallow in life is when you realize that not everyone is going to celebrate your successes and that there are some people that you allowed in your inner circle that don't even like you, but they are sitting around waiting for you to fall.

If you ever studied the life of Joseph, have you ever wondered why Joseph's brothers hated him enough to want him dead? It was more than just a dream, more than just a coat. It was even more than his father's apparent favoritism. They hated him because they realized that he was more than just a dreamer, but that he was a visionary—he was destined to be a great leader. They realized that his dreams were going to become a reality.

If the haters believe that your dreams and visions will not come fruition, they do not get upset—they might laugh or even feel sorry for you thinking that you are living on fantasy island. They will only get distressed and sip on hater-aid when deep inside they recognize that you are about to step into your destiny. The funny thing is that the haters see your potential before *you*. But don't allow haters to stop you from following your dreams. Joseph's brothers did not stop him from dreaming again.

In my life, my haters saw my potential and they hated on my God-given gifts and talents. They hated me, but still pimped me for my skills and abilities, and I allowed them to pimp me for my anointing. I would do things for people who did not like me, but I had such low self-esteem that when they asked me how much I charged, I would say 'nothing' or 'just give me what you want' which would usually equal nothing. When I finally began to realize my self-worth and tried to break the cycle, they tried to pull me back down. They would say things like 'don't forget where you came from,' but what they didn't understand is that I had spent a lifetime trying to forget my past. I had finally come to the realization that I had to forget my past in order to walk into my future. I had spent so many years walking backwards at times, and at other times I was walking forward, but looking backward.

Some people told me: *don't ever change, I adore you the way that you are.* When I was finally sick and tired of people using me and as I was struggling to free myself, what I started to realize is that what they meant is: *don't change because I can no longer control you; I cannot no longer profit off your low self-esteem.* Instead of helping me to conquer my fears, they wanted me to remain in prison.

I thought that I was happy being an encourager, but that was just a defense mechanism. Along the way I had allowed dream killers to kidnap my dreams and hold them hostage. After so many failures and mistakes, I was afraid to dream again. But there is something about when you begin to gain the courage to dream again that motivates you to start to revive your old dreams. When you say that I am going to step out of my history into destiny, there will be people who will try to stop you.

Don't give anyone in your history the power to control your future. There will come a time when you must wave bye baby to those people, places, and things that cannot support your greatness. This is not a dress rehearsal—you only get one chance at this thing called life. Therefore, there will come a day when you must be delivered from people and their opinion of you. I had to go through this deliverance process and free myself of people's opinions.

The same people that you thought you could depend on will be the same people that the devil will exploit to distract and discourage you. They will be the main ones whispering in your ear that you will never be able to write that book; who will read it? You are too old to go back to school; what are you going to do with a degree at your age? You cannot start a ministry; you are not that anointed.

They will say anything to keep you from your destination.

I had to make the declaration that I am not going to play this game anymore—I will not be a pawn in the devil's game. I was sick and tired of playing with the devil. I would make one move and then the devil would move and one-up me. And then I would make a move, but like in the game of chess, it was time for me to call checkmate, devil, the game is over.

One of the toughest pills for me to swallow is that there are a lot of people who have lost their dreams to murderers. There have been times in my life when God has planted something in my spirit or someone spoke a word over my life, and I was so excited that I could not wait to go and run and tell and share it with someone. I was depending on them being happy for me, that when the table turned and instead of encouragement, they discouraged me.

I went to them expecting a praise partner, but instead I found Debbie Downer, somebody that was mad because I still had a dream. I almost allowed them to kill my dreams. As a matter of fact, they thought that my dreams were dead. I even thought that they were dead, but they were not dead—they were in an induced coma and they were surviving on a ventilator.

Some people are satisfied in their comfort zone. They have become accustomed to living with lack and limitations.

They pretend that they are happy; they have convinced themselves that they are happy. They have become so accustomed to the struggle that they have adapted their life to living under such adverse conditions.

I can speak so candidly about people living in that state of mind because at the beginning of the writing of this book in August 2015, I was living in that state of mind.

I was satisfied with barely enough. I was appeased with living in my section eight apartment, working a two-cent job, and mad that I did not qualify for food stamps. I had allowed the dream killers to rock my dreams silently to sleep, but one day I woke up and looked around and discovered that I was no longer satisfied with my life. I asked myself why I was living beneath my means. My father owns all the cattle and land, why am I eating with the pigs? I was finally tired of accepting and eating the scraps off the table, tired of barely making it, sick and tired of being the tail and not the head. I was constantly shortchanging myself of the blessings of God. I once read this story about a man that had a lifelong dream to take a cruise: *There was once a man whose lifelong dream was to board a cruise ship and sail the Mediterranean Sea, He dreamed of walking the streets of Rome, Athens and Istanbul. He saved every penny until he had enough for his passage, since money was tight, he brought an extra suitcase and filled it with beans, boxes of crackers and bags of powdered lemonade and that's what he lived on every day. He would have loved to have taken part in the many activities. He yearned for only a taste of the amazing food he saw on the ship. But the man wanted to spend a very little bit of money that he did not participate in any of these. He could see the cities he had hoped to see but for the most part of journey he stayed in his cabin and ate only his humble food.*

On the last day of the cruise a crew members asked which ones of the farewell parties he was going to attend. It was then that he learned that not only was the farewell but almost everything on board the cruise ship. The food, the entertainment and almost all the activities had been included in the price of the ticket. It was too late when the man realized that he had been living beneath his privilege. ~ Author Unknown

I was tired of working like a slave 24/7, 365 days a year and still living beneath my means. I finally understood that somewhere along the road I had stopped dreaming. When you stop dreaming, you have no concept of what your future can be because sometimes you are so busy living in the past.

There comes a time when we must take all the adversity that we have gone through in life and make it an opportunity for growth. Wayne Gratz said, "You will always miss 100 percent of the shots that you do not take." I finally understood that my dreams were not dead, but that they were lying dormant. I thought that I was satisfied with my life the way that it was, but deep inside there was still a burning desire that would not allow me to stop dreaming. The reason that I knew my dreams were not dead is that I often would still speak of my dreams. The more that I spoke, the more the haters hated me; the more they hated me, the more I dreamed of a better life.

I just could not help it. I tried to accept my life, but I just wasn't satisfied. I was not pleased with my living conditions, my financial situation, even my ministry was not up to par. I believed God enough to understand that He had a plan for my life and this was not it. But what was it?

One test to know whether your dream is God-given, is if people can kill it, it is not God-given. When you have a dream that comes directly from the throne room of God, can't no dream killer sent from the pits of hell kill it. Every time the enemy sends an assassin to eradicate your dream, you dare to dream again. The assassin will follow you, stalk you, and take the time to catch you off guard to finally try to finish you off. But after each assassination attempt, I dared to dream again.

Joseph's dreams landed him in a pit, a palace, and eventually in a prison—all on his way from dreamer to visionary. Joseph was abused, used, and misunderstood—the dream killers tried their best to annihilate his purpose. Joseph shared his dreams with his family, but you must watch out for those dream killers, the ones that you share your secrets with.

There will be those that will whisper in your ear, 'how are you going to accomplish this or that?' You must have discernment concerning those you allow in your inner circle. You must wean out those who are always spreading negativity.

Be careful of those things that you accept because the enemy will send you those things that look good on the outside, but inside it's deception at its best. It was sent from the devil to destroy you. The enemy will send you a present all wrapped and pretty, but when you open it, it is filled with lies. You must be careful when you are pregnant with purpose. Giving birth is not easy, that is why you cannot have just anybody in the birthing room with you. You need midwives that are intercessors with clean hands and a pure heart. What God has conceived in you will come to pass this time because there will be no imposters in the delivery room.

I understand now the role that the enemy plays—the enemy comes to steal your inheritance and, in the process, he will attempt to destroy your faith in God. Let's examine the concept of kill and destroy. Often, when we think of the enemy coming to kill, we think that he comes to just kill our physical bodies.

But I dare you to delve deeper. Yes, it is true that the devil will afflict our bodies, but even more than physical death is the fatality of your dreams and visions. The enemy was content when he assumed that you were dead. He did not even mind you staring into space and daydreaming about better days, until you begin to make that move from dreamer to visionary.

There were people in my life that, when I embarked on the journey to achieving my dreams, those same people started to back away. The people who refused to go through the fire and the storm with me are not supposed to travel with me into my destiny. The people who believed in me when the pages of this book were blank—those are the people who will celebrate with me at the book signing.

I had to accept the fact that there are some people who come into my life for a season or a reason. Stop trying to hold on to what is killing you. They thought they were throwing me to the wolves, but what they did not know is that when they came back through, I would be driving the sled.

There is a familiar story about an old donkey that fell into a well: One day, a farmer's donkey fell into a well. The animal cried for hours and the farmer did not know what to do. He decided that the donkey was so old that it would not pay to get the donkey out of the well, so they decided to bury the donkey and they began to throw dirt. When they looked into the well, with each shovel of dirt the donkey was shaking it off, and packing it under his feet, and taking a step up until he was able to walk out of that well.

The trick to getting out of the well is to shake it off and take a step up. All your dream killers are stepping stones. Dream killers will always throw stones in the path of your success. It depends on *you* whether you will build a bridge or a wall. I had to build a bridge and let go of the people who wanted to walk away. I had to recognize who my dream killers were and to accept that it is okay to say farewell to those who were not meant to go to the next level with me. I was trying to bring people kicking and screaming into my destiny.

People who are meant to go all the way with you cannot leave, and those that are not meant to go cannot stay. God had to separate you from some people because the wrong associations will hinder your walk with God. Dream killers don't want to see you mature or change, or elevate to a new level. It is at this next level that you will go from dreamer to visionary.

The people that you want in your life are those that are positive; they believe in you even when you do not believe in yourself. They will do everything in their power to propel you to the next level.

The difference between my family and Joseph's family is that my family always recognized my gifts and talents. In my darkest hour when I thought all was lost, they believed in me. They continued to push me forwards toward my destiny. My family has always been my biggest cheerleaders. They continued to root for me through the storm and the rain, through the fire, and through every valley experience.

It was during this time that my other relationships had to stand the test of time. People who I thought would always be there for me began to walk away and scandalize my name. And there were others who I had questioned their loyalty, stepped up to the plate and encouraged me.

The enemy uses those who you thought was down for whatever, your ride or die, to distract you and try to sidetrack you. It is his motive and desire to kill your dream, your future, and your very desire to thirst for more out of your life.

Watch those dream killers—those that smile in your face. The O'Jays sang in the song, *Backstabbers*, "What they do, they smile in your face, but all the time they want to take your place. The back stabbers."

You also need to stay clear of the people who cannot see your vision—those who did not support you. Last year, while raising money for a scholarship fund in memory of my son, Tysean Thomas who died in February 2009, many people who said they loved me and my son and the cause, made promises and pledges that they could not uphold. I was so hurt and disappointed. This situation opened my eyes and made me realize that I could not depend on people to keep my dreams and visions alive.

Opposition has a way of refining and redefining you. The old cliché is that what doesn't kill you will make you stronger. God is working on you because He knows that He has placed something in you that can't no dream killers destroy. God will not allow any dream killers to rob you of your destiny, but God will set up something to propel you into your destiny.

People not supporting me in my scholarship efforts propelled me to write this book. It inspired me to stop dreaming and become a visionary. I saw my dreams almost die while I was making everyone else's dreams a reality.

Let's talk about Joseph again. The fact that Joseph's brothers sold him into slavery pushed him into his destiny. No dream killers could keep Joseph in the pit.

If people had not showed me their true colors while working on the scholarship, then I would have never gotten sick of people pimping me for my gifts and talents and not appreciating me. I was sick and tired of people not paying me what I was worth. This book would have never been written and, most importantly, I would not have been delivered from my past. This book was my deliverance tool; it was the vehicle that carried me from dreamer to visionary. I would have continued to live my life dissatisfied and empty, not really living, but merely existing.

The Bible tells us where there is no vision, where there are no new revelations, where there are no new dreams, the people perish. You cannot progress in what God has for you to do when you are not working towards your destiny. When you are not utilizing your gifts and talents, you will never be satisfied.

My secular job is teaching and I really enjoy working with children. I am passionate about education, but my real passion is writing and empowering women and young people that, despite circumstances and situations that you have gone through, God still has a plan for your life.

Along this windy road called life I have come face to face with many dream killers along the route. Some of us are the walking dead—the devil has killed our dreams and desires; we go through the motions but we are dead. The enemy does not want you to fulfill your purpose in life.

- What is your purpose?
- What are the desires of your heart?
- What is your why?
- What are the things that you long to do?
- If money wasn't an object, what would you be doing?

God has given you the ability to excel at something, the thing that you can use for the advancement of God's people. You need to focus your life around your strength. If the devil can destroy your purpose, then he can block, postpone, delay, or even try to abort your destiny. It is the desire of the enemy to kill you while you are still in your dreamer stage. He wants to prevent you from ever becoming a visionary.

For I know the plans I have for you declare the Lord. Plans to prosper you and not harm, plans to give you hope and the future (Jeremiah 29:11)

The expected end that the Lord has for you is your destiny. Destiny is a predestined course of events. The enemy wants to frustrate your purpose so you will never reach your expected end. Joseph had a dream and when he shared his dreams with his brothers, that is when the enemy crept into the mind and the heart of his brothers. You cannot tell everyone your dreams, even those that are close to you. Sometimes you must dream in secret, water it at the midnight hour with your tears. But what you have sowed in secret, you will certainly harvest it in front of your haters. My message to my haters is that if you cannot stand to see me blessed, then take a seat and watch what God is about to do in my life.

> *But as it is written Eye hath not seen, nor ears heard, neither have entered into the heart of man, this thing when God hath prepared for then that love him. (1 Corinthians 2:9)*

You need to identify and recognize what are your dream killers are. If you don't know what's killing your dreams, your dreams will continue to be buried in the valley of dead dreams and failed visions.

Chapter Three

The Valley of Dead Dreams and Failed Visions

"The season of failure is the best time for sowing seeds of success" ~ Paramahansa Yogananda

Everyone in life has had a dream at some time or another. Dreaming is a continual process and over the test of time, some dreams will change, some will fade away, and some will end up in the valley of dead dreams and failed visions. In the last chapter, we discovered that some of our dreams have fallen prey to dream killers.

There are several factors that can lead to the death of your dreams. One factor is people. People will kill your dreams if you allow them to.

There are accidental dream killers. Those are individuals who might really love and care about you, but unknowingly they will speak a word of discouragement that will deter you from following your dreams. The accidental dream killers might simply state the obvious. For example, ymight tell someone you want to write a book and the dream killers will simply state that it is hard to get a book published by a traditional publisher. You might share that you want to go back to school to finish your degree and they will ask, when will you have time to go back to school—you are a single parent, and you work a fulltime job and a part-time job.

When I went back to college to obtain my Bachelor's degree, I had a child and was working a fulltime and part time job, and was paying for my son to go to private school. The naysayers said I was not going to be able to accomplish it, but they were so wrong.

I would leave my fulltime job at Amityville Head Start at four o'clock and then I would go to Tutor Time down the street and would get off between six and seven. I would pick up my son and go to the library every night until it closed. I was on the school's parent committee and I could graduate in one year taking thirty- six credits. I was determined to get my degree and no dream killers could discourage me. The other type of dream killers are the deliberate dream killers.

These are individuals who are miserable in their own unproductive lives and don't want to see anyone else prosper.

Nonbelievers are people who don't believe that you can accomplish your dreams. Many nonbelievers have given up on their own dreams, therefore they are in no position to encourage anyone else to achieve their dreams.

You cannot allow people to stop you from chasing your dreams. Don't allow people to stop you from dreaming. People who you think that you can trust with your visions, and hope they will be in your corner—those are the very people that the enemy will use to destroy your dreams. The enemy will use them to distract you. The best defense is to avoid negative people. Many nonbelievers do not believe that you will ever accomplish your dreams. Many people will speak death to your dreams because they have long ago given up on their own dreams, therefore they are in no condition to encourage anyone else to strive toward their aspirations.

The best way to deal with people is to understand that you cannot share your dreams with everyone. Stop telling your dreams to everyone that you come across. Stop talking about your destiny and start walking into your destiny.

Sometimes it is our own fault that people have lost faith in our vision. For years they have heard us singing the same song about what we are going to do one day, and all they can smell is the stench that is coming from our personal valley of dead dreams and failed visions. The best course of action is to avoid these people.

Stay away from people who try to depreciate your dreams. Small minded people will always do that, but people who have a positive mindset will encourage you to reach for greatness. When you are aspiring to colossal things it is imperative that you associate with likeminded people.

"I think that it is important to get your surroundings as well as yourself into a positive state- meaning surround yourself with positive people, not the kind who are negative and jealous of everything you do." ~ *Heidi Klum*

Another factor is that we throw a pity party. People who constantly think 'woe is me' often have dead dreams. The lyrics from the song *Pity Party* by Melanie Martinez says, "It's my party and I'll cry if I want to. Cry if I want to. I'll cry until the candles burn down this place. I'll cry until my pity party is in flames." A pity party is the way that you show grief over the course of your life. You are also complaining about how bad your life is. Pity parties can be just for one, or sometimes you will invite people that will share in your misery. The cliché, misery likes company, is true in this case.

One of the people who is almost certain to attend a pity party is the enemy and all his imps. At the party, we dress in our pajamas and think of all our 'if onlys'—my life would have been different if only I would have stayed in school and not gotten pregnant at an early age; if only I had never gone to that party, I would have never gotten raped; if only I would have told someone that my stepfather was molesting me, it would have stopped; if only I had never told anyone that he was molesting me then my family would not have been torn apart; if only I had never married him I would have never suffered years of physical abuse. Our lives are filled with 'if onlys' and all our 'if onlys,' pains, regrets, mistakes and failures can destroy our ability to dream.

When we can't get over our past mistakes, we often stay locked in our yesterdays. We will find that we are locked into a prison like Joseph. The difference between our prison and Joseph's is that Joseph was in a physical prison and our prison is a mental one. This prison originates in your mind; you feel worry, fear, and hopelessness. We feel that our life is hopeless and that there is no need for us to ever dream again.

It is God's desire to free you from your mental prison of locked up dreams and desires. God wants to free you from the valley of dead dreams and failed visions. Today you can begin to overcome any negative thoughts and live a life full of hopes and dreams.

> *Do not be conformed to this world. But be transformed by the renewal of your mind, that by testing you may discern what is the will of God, and what is good and acceptable and perfect. (Romans 12:1-2)*

A lot of people do not realize that the reason why they are not happy and the reason why they are not achieving their dreams, is because they have trained their mind to think in the wrong direction. We often say that we cannot put God in a box, but God is not in a box—often it is us in the box. In the box is our comfort zone; we are safe in our box. When things don't happen the way that we feel they should, we think if 'I keep trying eventually something might work out for me.' Little by little, discouragement, doubt, and defeat will creep in. These negative thoughts will become your standard way of living. It's time to cut off the music, the party is over.

Another factor that can lead to dead dreams is laziness. The truth be told is that many people do not achieve their dreams because they are too lazy to put forth any efforts in achieving their dreams. The state of laziness has killed many dreams, careers, and futures. I don't know how people think they are going to achieve anything in life just being plain ole lazy. The state of being lazy means that we are not willing to get up early, stay up late, and work hard to get where we want to be.

When you are trying to chase your dreams, you have to stay on your grind. You have to work just as hard or harder on your dreams that you do on your 9 to 5 job. There are circumstances that you might go through in life that might cause you to put your dreams on the back burner. Maybe you got pregnant at an early age and had to drop out of school, and after years of working to make ends meet, you were too lazy to put forth the effort to go back to school and to work.

> *"Know the true value of time; snatch, seize and enjoy every moment of it. No idleness, no laziness, no procrastination: never put off till tomorrow what you can do today." ~ Philip Stanhope*

Most of us have had some lazy days in our lives, days when we just want to sleep the day away or maybe even the week, but most of the time it is a temporary state; it is not permanent and then we snap out of it and move on to pursue our dreams and aspirations. But what happens when we lose our determination and motivation to go after our dreams? The Bible speaks of laziness in Proverbs:

> *How long will you lie down sluggard when will you arise from your sleep, a little sleep, a little slumber, a little folding of hands to rest, your poverty will come*

in like a vagabond and you need like an armed man. (Proverbs 6: 9-11)

Laziness separates us from our own potential. People who are lazy refuse to press on in seasons of dryness. The lazy person would rather give up than work hard to achieve their goals and aspirations. Working hard takes a determined mindset. You have to train yourself to want to work hard.

"Inspiration is a guest that does not willingly visit the lazy." ~ Pyotr Ilyich Tchaikovsky

Another factor that can lead to your dreams ending up in the valley of dead dreams and failed visions is procrastination. Procrastination is putting off or postponing something for a later time.
It is avoiding a task in favor of doing something more pleasurable. I will go on a diet next week. I will go back to school next month. Next year I will start my own business. Procrastination is a tool that the enemy will use to keep you from achieving your dreams. Throughout our lifetimes we will have a

tremendous amount of ideas, but we will fail to act on them. We all procrastinate at times.

Procrastination is a killer. It will kill your productivity, dreams, motivation, and ambitions. If we continue to put off and make excuses, we will never achieve our best life ever.

You can destroy procrastination by setting small goals and objectives. In the Bible, there were four lepers that sat at the door of the city procrastinating as they decided what their next move was going to be:

And there were four leprous men at the entrance of the gate, and they said one to another, why sit here and die? If we say that we enter the city, then the famine is in the city, and we shall die there, and if we sit here, we die also. Now therefore come, and if we fall unto the host of the Syrians; if they save us alive, we shall live; and if they kill us, we shall but die. And they rose in the twilight to go into the camp of the Syrians, and when they come to the uttermost part of the camp of Syria behold there was no man there. (2 Kings 7:3-5)

These men, as they sat procrastinating, they faced certain death, but as soon as they decided to act, God provided a miracle for them. It is time for you to arise and take action. What dreams have you not pursued because you are still waiting on tomorrow to come? What dreams have you put on hold because of past mistakes?

There is a process that you must go through to achieve your goals. Please do not allow hurdles and obstacles to stop you from following your dreams. The only cure for procrastination is action. Talking about it or thinking about it will not get you anywhere, unless they are followed by action. Procrastination is a choice—we choose whether or not we are going to act. Procrastination can make you unhappy; you are unhappy with the life that you are living, but you lack the motivation and the determination to take the first step.

"I'd be more frightened by not using whatever abilities I have been given. I'd be more frightened by procrastination and laziness." ~ Denzel Washington.

Finances are another dream killer:

"If you are born poor, it's not your mistake, but if you die poor, it's your mistake." ~ Bill Gates

It is important that we look at our lives and the life that we really want to live. See where you are at now and where you desire to go. Where exactly are you now in achieving your dreams? Have you achieved your goals and aspirations?

We have discovered that procrastination is a dream killer, so the best time to start is now. It is time to build a bridge and get over those things that might be hindering you whether it is time, experience, or money. The mere fact that you have a dream is making you one step closer to success. Having a God-given dream will push you and motivate you towards your goals when circumstances and situations arise.

One of the biggest obstacles that hinder people from achieving their dreams is resources and finances. You often think that you will never have enough money to finance your dreams.

It is imperative that you invest in yourself. Investing in yourself will get you one step closer to achieving your goals. It is your mindset that needs to change in regards to investing in yourself.

At tax time, people will spend thousands of dollars being ghetto fabulous, buying Michael Kors and Prada, but will declare they do not have money to invest in their dreams. They will spend hundreds of dollars on hair weaves and nails, but don't have the money to invest in their dreams. You must invest in your dreams.

You must think about it every minute of the day. You must walk, talk, and live your dreams. Success comes with sacrifices. When you are working towards your dreams you might have to cook at home and give up going out to dinner. Maybe this year you might have to invest your vacation money in your dreams. If you do not believe in your dreams enough to invest in them, no one else is going to invest in them. It's your dream, your baby, and you must invest more into your dream than anyone else. No one owes you anything, the only person that owes you anything is you. Investing in yourself is the most profitable thing that you can ever do.

We often feel because of family obligations that investing in yourself is selfish. If you want a better life then you must first invest in yourself. One of the ways that you can invest in yourself is to buy books and study the subject that you are interested in and research. Write out your vision and what you need to complete your goals.

And the Lord answered me and said Write the vision, make it plain upon tables, that he may run that readeth it. (Habakkuk 2:2)

In the valley of dead dreams and failed visions is low self-esteem. Low self-esteem will prevent you from dreaming at all. Low self-esteem kills aspirations. It will affect how you view your future. If you do not believe that you deserve better in life, you will not strive for better. At the very core of low self-esteem are your personal feelings of being inadequate and not being good enough. You never feel worthy enough, you never felt good enough. You struggle with insecurity and you feel worthless, but you do things for other people and allow them to take advantage of you. You are a people pleaser and seek their approval.

For years, I suffered from this condition. I would go over and above to please people and I would allow them to take advantage of me and pimp my gifts and talents.

For most of my life, I lacked confidence in myself and my abilities. I didn't believe I could achieve the things that I desired in life. I wanted to be a writer, but I thought it would be too hard to get published, and if I did get published, who would read it? And if I self-published, it would cost too much money.

I was always feeling frustrated because it hurt to want something so badly, yet not believe I could do it. Wanting it so badly, but being scared to start. These feelings were limiting my potential in life. I had to find a way to combat these feelings and start to live my best life ever.

I was not born with these insecurities, but dream killers started whispering negative thoughts in my ears as a child. That's why it's important that we watch what we say to children because they will internalize what you call them and they will act like what you say they are. When we say that 'you are just like your deadbeat father,' we change their character traits. Parents, be careful what you call your children. Be careful of calling them idiots or stupid because it hurts and can damage them for a lifetime. If you tell a child that he will never amount to anything, it won't be long before they begin to believe it. Some of us came from homes where we were called nasty names. For many years I thought

I was a jezebel before I found out what a jezebel is, and I was far from a jezebel, slut, or whore.

To build up your confidence, you must know who you are. It is important that you identify your strengths and weaknesses, and once you identify those, then you need to pinpoint your passions. Do the things that you are strong in and make you happy. For example, you might be an excellent teacher, but if you don't like children then teaching is not the field for you. Your strengths and your passion need to line up, and that will give you the confidence that you need to succeed.

The thing that built up my confidence was when I was chosen to be a part of an anthology called *Love, Marriage and Divorce*. I wrote the segment 'Divorce' and the responses that I received gave me the confidence to start writing this book.

> *Confidence comes from success, but confidence also combines another quality because you can be successful yet lack confidence. It requires a mental attitude*

shift to an expectation of success. And this alone can bring about more success, reinforcing the confidence it spirals from there." ~ Jason Hihn

Another factor that can lead your dreams to the valley of dead dreams and failed visions is excuses. Excuses are rationalizations that we make to defend our behaviors. Excuses are dream killers when we have an excuse for why we cannot achieve our dreams. Your downfalls in life are never your fault, but it is always someone else's fault. You must work to take care of your family so you don't have the time to chase your dreams. You are not educated enough to go back to school. You live paycheck to paycheck so you don't have the money to invest in your dreams. Excuses.

Excuses will kill your dreams. We make excuses for many reasons. Like fear of embarrassment. Fear of failure. We make excuses when things do not turn out the way that we expected. For example, you fail a test that you did not prepare for—instead of owning up to the fact that you did not study, your excuse is the professor put things on the test that were not supposed to be on the test. We try to explain why we should have, could have, or would have done something that we failed to do.

A common excuse is: I don't know how. I would write a book, but I don't know how to write a book. You must learn how to do it—study, practice, investigate the knowledge you need to complete the task.

A big excuse is: I have been like this all my life. I cannot change. This simply means that you do not have the motivation and determination to change. It's time to stop making excuses and start to live the life God intended for you to live.

He that is good at making excuses is seldom good for anything else. ~ Benjamin Franklin.

One of the main dream killers is your past. You are so busy looking backwards that you cannot look ahead to your future.

Brethren I count myself to have apprehended: but this one thing I do, forgetting those things that are behind me, and reaching forth unto those things which are before me, I press toward the mark of the prize of the high calling of God in Christ Jesus.
(Philippians 3:13-14)

Paul in this scripture declares that I am not all that I should be, but I am focusing on forgetting my past and looking forward to what lies ahead. The Apostle Paul had been through a lot in his life. He experienced a major transformation in his life when he went from the biggest persecution of the church to one of the greatest church planters and authors in the New Testament. He had a lot of haters inside and outside of the church.

Not everyone is happy when you change your life. You cannot allow your past failures, hurts, mistakes, and disappointments to stop you from experiencing God's best for you today. For many of us today, our past is holding us hostage. Your past is the experiences that have played a role in making you who you are. It might be emotional hurts, personal pain, rejection, and disappointments. Many people are in bondage because of their past. They are in a state of stagnation because they cannot move from their past.

We often permit the pain from our past to continue to guide us in our present and predetermine our future. Everyone has memories and our memories can either be friend or foe. We carry baggage from our past that loads us down. Packed in our suitcase is guilt, depression, and fear. Carrying these heavy loads will weigh you down.

The devil, the father of all lies, will whisper in your ear that even God doesn't love you, and you deserve all the bad things that happened to you. You are so bad that you are not worthy of God's love. You will never be able to change and you will never be able to break the chains that hold you to your past.

Society has shaped the way that we feel about the correlation between our past and our future. Studies have shown that people who grow up in abusive homes, whether it is physical, verbal, or sexual, will grow up to be abusive. If your mother was a teenage parent, then you will be a teenage mom. If your parents were alcohol or drug abusers, you will grow up to be an alcoholic or drug addict. Psychologists use the term *cycle of abuse* to describe this vicious cycle. We repeat the mistakes from our past repeatedly.

Many of us have skeletons in our closet and the enemy will keep opening the door allowing them to fall out. Many of us spend so much of our precious time looking back and regretting our past, that we fear the future. We spend so much time in the past, we push the replay button and we replay our past repeatedly. When we tell our life stories we tell of the pain, of how someone betrayed us, or the loss of a loved one—we remember the past pain more than we do the positive things. A life story full of failure, mistakes, and regrets. There are things that happened to us in our past that still hurts us; we can still feel the residue. But despite all of that, there is hope to close the door on your past mistakes and failures; you can move from victim to victor. Let's look at Joseph's life again. Joseph's story is full of hope, promises, purpose, physical, mental sufferings, and the ultimate betrayal from his family. Joseph lived through the most adverse of conditions and he survived.

He was an overcomer. Joseph was tried and tested to what should have been his breaking point, but he reached beyond the break and held on. He never lost his integrity and he never blamed God for his past. Most importantly, he never allowed his past to dictate his future. Joseph understood that his present situation was not his destination.

"You build on failure. You can use it as a stepping stone. Close the door on the past. You don't try to forget the mistakes, but you don't dwell on them. You don't let them

have any of your energy, or any of your time, or any of your space." ~ *Johnny Cash*

Another factor that can lead to your dreams being in the valley of dead dreams and failed visions is the fear of failure. The fear of failure is the fear of failing and rejection. The fear of failure will stop you from doing the things that will help you to achieve your goals. Failure is something that is not uncommon to humans. We will all fail at something at one time or another in our lives. All of us have a fear of failing: What if I try this and it doesn't work?

Fear is one of the strongest tactics in the enemy's arsenal. The enemy will originate the fear in your mind and blow it up out of proportion to make you believe that failure is only unique to you. The enemy will make you feel small and inadequate. The fear of failure can stagnate you and paralyze you. The fear of failure will make you too scared to even try. The enemy will whisper sweet nothings in your ear and tell you that you will never change, that you are not an overcomer, that you will not make it through this. You will never be victorious in any area of your life.

Fear will keep you in your comfort zone. We will convince ourselves that we are happy in our present situation. We tend to take failure personally and we feel that failure defines who we are, expresses our character. We interpret failure to mean that we are not good enough. Fear of failure can have its roots in many different things such as having parents that did not support you as a child. When you are not supported as a child, you carry these destructive thoughts into adulthood. Another cause can be failing at something that you were passionate about and you tried it, but you failed at it and after that you did not want to try anymore. Fear of failure is not a new phenomenon, it been around since biblical days.

So I was afraid and I went out and hid your talent in the ground, see here what belongs to you. His master replied you wicked, lazy servant! So, you knew that I harvest where I have not sown and gather where I have not scattered seed? Well then you should have put my money on deposit with the bankers, so that when I returned I would have received it back with interest. (Matthew 25: 25-27)

In this parable, Jesus wants us to know that when we live in fear, we do not live by faith.

"Failure is so important. We speak about success all the time. It is the ability to resist failure or use failure that often leads to greater success. I've met people who do not want to try for fear of failing." ~ JK Rowling

The fear of failure is so strong and pungent that we sabotage our chances at success. The fear of failure can trigger feelings such as disappointment, anger, and regret. The fear of failure will make you value other people's opinions of you more highly than your own. You will begin to accept other people's thoughts of you and allow them to identify you. The fear of failure will have you doubting your abilities, gifts, and talents.

In order to avoid the pits and to avoid the valley of dead dreams and failed visions, you have to overcome your fear of failure. It is impossible to go through your entire life without ever failing at something. It's all in how we view the failure; it is our mindset. Failure can be a learning experience, or the reason why we throw in the towel. We need to look at the experience and learn something from it. We need to mature and grow. We do not want to continue to make the same mistake repeatedly.

There are many famous people that failed at something in their lives, but they did not allow it to stagnate them. Michael Jordan was cut from his high school basketball team because the coach did not feel that he was good enough. I wonder how that coach feels now. Warren Buffet did not get into Harvard and now he is one of the richest business men in America. Most of us will fall and hurt our knees, but we do not stay down there. Just think of what would have happened if Michael Jordan had allowed that coach to speak death to his dreams and never picked up a basketball again.

When you fail, it can teach you how strong you really are. If I had never failed I would never know my own strength. When we decide to do any type of venture we understand that there is a fifty-fifty chance that we might just fail. We worry about how we are going to fund our vision. Am I really qualified for this? Can my dreams really happen? I know what God promised me. Can my dreams live?

I am beginning to overcome the fear of failure and my dreams will not die in the valley of dead dreams and failed visions because dreams delayed are not dreams denied.

Chapter Four

Dreams Delayed Are Not Dreams Denied

And let us not get weary in well doing: for in due season we shall reap if we faint not. (Galatians 6:9)

Once we have resuscitated our dreams and rescued our dreams from the valley of dead dreams and failed visions, sometimes we still become discouraged and feel like our dreams are never going to happen. Sometimes God may delay the fulfilling of your dreams. Many of us have pondered in our hearts whether the promises of God will ever be manifested in our lives.

Delay is also one of the tactics of the enemy because he wants you to doubt God. The enemy wants you to believe that your dreams will never come true. But God will use periods of waiting to teach us to be more patient. We are a microwave generation and we desire instant gratification. Sometimes our dreams are delayed for God to let us know what is really in our hearts because He already knows, but He wants us to realize it.

> *"And thou shalt remember all the way which the Lord thy God led thee these forty years in the wilderness, to humble thee, and to prove thee, to know what was in thine heart, whether thou wouldest keep his commandment, or no. (Deuternomy8:2)*

Most the time dreams are not fulfilled instantly, but there is always a waiting period. God will use the waiting period to prepare us for what He has in store for us.

But what often happens while we are waiting is that those same dream killers will resurface if we have not destroyed them at the root.

The first dream killer that will rear its ugly head again is fear. When God delivered the children out of Egypt with all the difficult circumstances that they had to endure, they lost their faith and began to have fear.

> *Whither shall we go up? our brethren have discouraged our heart, saying, the people is greater and taller than we; the cities are great and walled up to heaven; and moreover, we have seen the sons of the Anakims there. (Deuteronomy 1:28)*

They desperately wanted to be free so they were not afraid to leave Egypt, but along the way fear set in and they were afraid to enter the promised land.

One of the problems with fear is that fear will keep you in your wilderness experience and it delays the fulfilling of your purpose. Many of us have not accomplished our dreams because we are afraid to step out in faith.

When we are in our wilder-ness we tend to start to think that God has forgotten us. It can be very unsatisfying when you try and your dreams are still on the backburner of life.

Dreams delayed are not dreams denied; you must never give up on yourself and, more importantly, never give up on the promises of God. If God said it, it must come to pass.

I know at times while you are waiting on your dreams, you will feel defeated and those feelings of unworthiness will resurface. During these times, we must encourage ourselves and realize that giving birth is not easy. The harder the struggle, the bigger the dream. When we are birthing something that will change people's lives, the birthing process will not be easy.

Sometimes our dreams are delayed because we are not in a position to receive them. We are not ready for the dream. To be a great leader there are several qualities that you must possess. One is a positive attitude. To have your followers happy and motivated you must display a positive attitude. You must be resilient. You must know how to cope with catastrophes and setbacks.

In the pursuit of God-given dreams, you will face windy roads filled with hurdles, obstacles, dead ends, and delays. Many times on route, our spiritual GPS will say 'rerouting.' There will be times that we will find that we have journeyed so far from our dreams.

Let's look at Joseph's life again. Early in his life, Joseph had great dreams, but those dreams were delayed. In life, we will go through many different seasons. We cannot escape hard times. No matter how saved we are, we are going to face adversity. There will be challenges and suffering. No matter how hard we pray there will be times that everything we touch seems to turn to stone. There are times that we will go through things that we are not meant to change, but we are meant to go through it. There are times when we need to wait on God.

For the vision is yet for an appointed time, but at the end it shall speak, and not lie: though it tarry, wait for it, because it will surely come, it will not tarry. (Habakkuk 2:3)

In life, we often wrestle with the idea of waiting on God. We realize that we have an appointment with our destiny, but we do not want to wait—we want our name to be called right away. An appointment is a meeting that is already set up. When we go to the doctor, we either have an appointment or we are a walk-in. The person with the appointment knows exactly what time their appointment is, and a walk-in is seen when all the appointments are over. But sometimes, even when we have an appointment, we are not called at the exact time of our appointment. We still must wait.

Have you ever noticed that people react differently to the same situation? Some people while they are waiting will grow more focused, while others will fall apart during the waiting process. The way that we respond to our waiting season depends on the perspective in which we view things. God has a purpose for all our lives and our steps are predestined by God. We cannot allow our situations and circumstances to make us lose focus on the purpose that God has for our lives. The enemy will try to delay what God has spoken over our lives, but the weapons that he forms will not prosper.

We must realize that God's blessings do not always come in the way that we expect them to come and it will not come through the people that you thought would have your back. Sometimes when we realize that the people that we thought would be there for us are not, then we end up in a state of brokenness. The hard times that we face in life can either develop us or break us—it is up to us which one we choose. We must understand that when God wants to prepare us for the purpose that He has for us, He does not send us to the college of ease, but rather to the college of hard knocks.

Joseph came to the throne in Egypt by way of the pit and the dungeon. As Joseph sat in a lonely cell for a crime that he did not commit, the days turned into weeks, and the weeks into months, and the months into years. Can you imagine him sitting in the cell thinking about the dreams and visions that God had given him? Him thinking about his jealous brothers that sold him into slavery, but deep down they really wanted him dead? Then after all that dysfunction in his life, Potiphar's wife lies on him and slanders his name. His character is in question and that very lie is what has him sitting in a cold, hard cell asking God, 'Where are you, can you even hear my prayers? I don't understand it, but God I believe you.'

When we suffer like Joseph did, sometimes we feel like God has forgotten us, but we cannot allow our past situations to abort our future opportunities. In life, we are going to face broken places, failures, and mistakes in life. Failures do not mean that I will never make it—it only means that I must try a little harder. Failure does not mean that God has forgotten me—it just means that you have something bigger for me, that my dreams were not big enough.

There are several categories of people in life. There are the drop-outs—those who give up on their dreams and never take responsibility. It is always someone else's fault. Then there are the cop-outs—those that make excuses for why they stop dreaming. And there are the hold-outs—the ones that waited too long to go after their dreams. And then there are the all-outs—those that go all out for their dreams, and when they fail they do not give up, but they continue to chase after their dreams.

Suffering will come. Things will come that will knock the wind out of you. Do not allow it to take you out, but allow it to propel you higher.

Allow it to make you rise to the occasion. God never promises us that we would not face challenges in life, but He did not mean for these challenges to kill us. He meant for them to make us want to dream bigger. It is important at this point to remember that if a dream is God-given, it will face opposition. Joseph dreamt big dreams for himself and even though Joseph's dreams were God-given they did not happen overnight, but they were delayed. The morning after Joseph woke up from his dream, he probably felt like he was ready to walk into his destiny.

Sometimes our dreams are delayed because we are not ready for that position yet. Leaders must possess certain skills. To be an effective leader, you must be competent. Competence is the ability to do a job and do that job well. You cannot lead people to a place where you have never been yourself. Another trait that you need is character. Character is who you are when no one is looking. Your character is who you are as a person. A leader must be reliable, honest, and trustworthy.

Joseph had the potential to be a great leader, but he was not ready yet to acquire the position. Joseph had to come to a place of humbling. In the scriptures, we saw that he had no problem running back to his father and telling on his brothers. You do not have to belittle someone else to make yourself look big. Perhaps Joseph, already knowing that he was favored by his father, maybe he wanted to ensure that position in his father's life; so he brought back a bad report to damage his brothers' reputation and for him to continue to be the golden child. Perhaps Joseph is like the coworker who watches and waits for you to make a mistake so they can report you to the boss and prove that you are not perfect. Or they might want to make you look incompetent so they can have your job or be next in line for a promotion. Whatever the reason, they are more than happy to sell you up the river.

Joseph already understood that his brothers did not like him because of their father's favoritism towards him. Many of us will not be liked just because of the favor that we have over our lives. Even though Joseph knew how his brothers felt about him, he still did not hesitate to share his dreams that he would one day rule over them time and time again. There were still some things in Joseph that had to be purged out of him before he was ready for his dreams to be manifested.

DREAM KILLERS

If God has placed a vision in your heart, but you have not yet stepped into your destiny, examine your heart and your motives. Maybe there is a pruning that must take place in your life. There are some character traits that you cannot take with you to your greater purpose. Maybe you need to build up your competence in one area or another, or you might have a character flaw or two that you need to work on. We cannot take always make excuses and blame others for our stagnation; sometimes we must realize that it is us.

As I examined my life and questioned why I was stuck between dream and manifestation, I came to the cold hard realization that my delay was contingent upon me and my mindset. I had to begin with a total transformation of my thinking process and release my stinking thinking. I had to release my worrying about people and what they thought about me. I was a people pleaser and you cannot seek to please people and please God at the same time. People are wishy-washy. They will love you one minute and when you do not beat to their drums, they will hate you the next minute.

I had to go through a humbling experience when I had to realize that it was not about me and my feelings, but it is about the kingdom of God and building that Kingdom, not my own selfish agenda. I also had to realize that my time is not God's timing, so our dreams are delayed because it is just not our time yet. In Joseph's case, it was just not his time yet to step into the position that God had already predestined for him. It was at a time that Joseph needed to be in a leadership position so he could be in the position to help his family during the famine. It is all about God's timing and God's timing does not always coincide with our timing.

God-given dreams don't just happen by happenstance, but they come through persistence, determination, and motivation—never giving in, giving up, or giving out.

You must be careful who you share your dreams with. Telling your dreams to the wrong people can land you in a pit. Not everyone is going to have the same relationship that you have with God, or possess the same measure of faith that you have. God gives us dreams and visions to accomplish in life and as soon as we share it, here comes the dream killers to oppose, suppress, and even try to kill our dreams.

You must keep the faith even when you are in your pit. Don't get comfortable in your pit because you are on the way to the palace. Along the way from promise to purpose you will certainly have to fight spiritual battles. The enemy will launch an all-out attack against you. Sickness will come. You will experience financial attacks and mental attacks on your mind—these are all attacks from the enemy that come straight from the pit of hell.

But our greatest attacks will come from people who have eyes, but cannot see what you see; ears, but cannot hear what you hear. They are haters and they hate you because you are not satisfied where you are and that you refuse to remain in that same condition. They tolerate you as long as you don't have anything and don't want anything, but when you get a glimpse of your destiny and you grab a hold of your dream and you get so excited that you want to share your news with everybody, those that you share your news with become resentful and critical of your dreams.

If Joseph could have only kept his mouth closed, if only I could have kept my mouth closed, I would have never met the dream killers. But there is something about a God-given dream—you cannot just let it die. One thing that I learned is that when you are anointed by God and you have the favor of God over your life and you have a God-given dream, you are going to have enemies and you will go through pit experiences, and during these experiences it will appear like your dreams have been denied.

During these pit experiences, we might feel like we are never going to make it out of the pit alive, but you will survive your pit experience. Don't settle there; start packing your bags, forward your mail to your next address—and your next address is the palace. You are destined for the palace; the pit is preparing you for your purpose. The pit was a delay, not a denial, but it is just a chapter in your life.

A chapter is a period. There is a beginning and ending to your chapter, and each chapter leads to another chapter. Some chapters are longer than others. Some chapters are good and some are bad, some are happy and others are sad. I am sure that as Joseph went through the many different chapters in his life, at one point or the other he might have felt like God had forgotten him. And at certain points in our lives, we too have thought just maybe God has forgotten us. People have lied on us; we have been rejected by people who felt like we would never amount to anything. You have been betrayed, talked about, and had your heart broken too many times to remember, and many of us have been thrown in a pit and left to die.

It was the intention of the enemy to kill us both spiritually and eventually, naturally. The enemy wants us to believe that God has denied all our prayers and petitions. The enemy wants to kill the dreamer that resides inside of you because the enemy recognizes that if he can kill your dreams and the dreamer in you, then he has already defeated you and rendered you helpless.

It is time to renew your mind. The renewal of your mind is a process. It is the process of changing your mindset. It is taking all doubts, fears, and hurts and turning your pain into your purpose. Renewing your mind is not simply just changing your thought pattern, but it is putting on the mind of Christ Jesus.

> *I beseech you therefore, brethren, by the mercies of God that you present your body a living sacrifice, holy, acceptable to God, which is your reasonable service and be not conformed to this world, but by the transformed by the renewing of your mind, that you may prove what is that good and acceptable and perfect will of God. (Romans 12:1-2)*

Everything begins in our mind and that is the reason why the adversary wants to attack our mind.

It is the enemy's most used weapon. That is why it is important that we recognize who the enemy is, what his weapons of mass destruction are, and you must learn how to counteract his attack. You must understand that it is your responsibility to renew your mind. You can find a strategy for renewing your mind in Philippians:

Finally, brethren, whatsoever things are true, whatsoever things are honest, whatsoever things are just, whatsoever things are pure, whatsoever things are lovely, whatsoever things are of good report; if there be any virtue, and if there be any praise, think on these things. Those things, which ye have both learned, and received, and heard, and seen in me, do: and the God of peace shall be with you. (Philippians 4:8-9)

We need to put off our old way of thinking and develop a new way of thinking. What do you want to concentrate on and think about?

Joseph was pushed in a pit and eventually sold into slavery by his brothers. He was lied on and ended up in prison; seemingly all hope was gone, but God had a plan for his life—and not just the plan for his life, but also for his family's salvation. During all the years between his dream and the manifestation of his dream, I do not recall any scriptural account of him being bitter; and he was rejected, lied on, and misused, but he never blamed anyone for the injustices that he faced in life. Many years later, when he came face to face with his brothers again, they were afraid that he was going to seek revenge for how they had treated him earlier in life, but what he did was remarkable and the epitome of someone with a renewed mind. He told his bothers that 'you wanted to hurt me, you wanted to destroy me, but God intended it for good, not only to save me but to save the lives of many people.'

But as for you, ye thought evil against me; but God meant it unto good, to bring to pass, as it is this day, to save much people alive." (Genesis 50: 20)

Joseph could have had unforgiveness in his heart and when he saw his brothers, He could have plotted revenge against them and saw this as an opportunity to throw in his brothers' face that many years he told them that they were going to need him and that he was going to rule over them.

I can identify with Joseph. I grew up in what society would describe as dysfunctional. My mother was a single parent with five children. But just as the Lord was with Joseph, through all that I have gone through—the abuse, rejection, and failures—God has been with me. God is with you, and God has not forgotten you. I know as you go through seasons in your life the enemy will whisper in your ear that God has forgotten you and that your dreams have been denied. God has not forsaken you and God is not punishing you. God has a bigger purpose for our lives and we cannot see it as we are going through our pits, delays, and detours in life. God is painting a bigger picture than the one that I visualized. I was using watercolors, but he was designing a masterpiece.

Situations and circumstances do not define your character or your destiny in life. We cannot continue to delay our destiny because we are so busy thinking about our past and what happened to us in the past—who lied on you, who slanders your name—and we spend so much time talking about our haters that we allow them to consume us.

We spend valuable time, when we should be chasing our dreams, worrying about unnecessary things. I do not in any way want to minimize the pain and hurt that you have gone through because I understand that it hurt, and it hurt like hell, but what I am saying is to reach for your destiny.

Many things that happen to us in life we do not deserve it and it is not your fault, but you no longer want to be a victim—you want to be a victor.

Joseph did not give up when he was thrown in the pit. He did not give up in the prison and because of his faithfulness, God promoted him to the Palace.

You also must remember that your circumstances in life do not define you. Everyone in life goes through valley experiences, but it is not what you go through that defines you, it is what is inside of you.

The enemy wants you to believe that your present situation is your destination, but the devil is a liar. People will try to define you and plan your failure and your demise, and many are sitting around waiting for you to fail.

Joseph went down as low as anybody could go and was hurt by the people who were supposed to be in his corner—his family. But through it all, he understood that delay was not denial. He went from riches to rags back to riches.

He went from suffering to success, from prison to a palace, from dreamer to visionary. Sometimes in our lives, our dreams will run off course and take detours. Sometimes we take the wrong roads and it seems like we will never get back on course. Some detours are orchestrated by God to build something in us and other detours we bring upon ourselves because of doubts and fear. Some people's dreams are delayed because they have unrealistic expectations and when they cannot live up to those expectations, they give up and doubt that God ever gave them that dream. Some people try to live up to other people's expectations and the limits that they put on them. It is time to think out-side of the box; do not allow anyone to box you into thinking small.

We are often our own worst enemy. In life, we are going to go through some hard trials on the way to our dreams and some of these things are going to knock the wind out of us, but we are not knocked out. It is time, my friend, to awaken the dreamer in you. Like Joseph, you might have been stripped of your coat, you might have lost your job, you might be going through a nasty divorce, you might have lost your home, you might have even lost your faith for a while. You might have even let hate fester in your heart.

I recall a very dark period in my life when I was betrayed by people that were supposed to be my friends. I moved into one of my friend's mother's house and went through a lot of changes with these so-called friends, so I ended up homeless with my two children. And I had hatred in my heart for them. I was in the pulpit still preaching, but from a place of hurt—and hurt people hurt other people.

One day I was so sick and tired of the hate that I had in my heart that was keeping me from achieving my dreams and living the life that God has ordained for me, and I came to the hard realization that I was dirty and I so desperately wanted to be clean. I remember running to the altar, making my own altar call with hot tears flowing down my face and a longing just to be closer to God.

At that time in my life, I did not care who was looking at me and I did not care what they thought about me. I just wanted to be free and I started to sing my own version of 'I say yes, Lord, yes to your will and to your way and when the spirit speaks to me with my whole heart, I will be free and the answer will be yes, oh yes.' I could not wait until the end of service. I could not wait for the clergy to make the altar call. The order of service was not important. I just wanted the chains off of me. I wanted to be free.

That was a dark chapter in my life, but it was not my final chapter. In that chapter, I was broken, humiliated, sad, and miserable, but my story did not end there. Somebody else who is reading this book went through a dark chapter in their life and the enemy might have told you that it was over, that all your dreams have been denied, but I wrote this chapter in transparency to encourage that the devil is a liar and your delay was not a denial. Your pit was not permanent. You are not going to perish in the pit; the pit was only a temporary setback. Your dream cannot be contained in a pit because your dream is bigger than the pit. Oh yeah, it is true that the enemy thought you were going to die in the pit. He laughed as he pushed you in, thinking that you were facing certain death. But how many of you know that the enemy cannot kill what God has predestined to live?

No matter what the enemy desires to steal from you, he cannot take the anointing of God from out of your life. Joseph was in the pit, but he was still anointed. He was in the palace and his integrity was tested and he was lied on, but he was still anointed. He was sent to a dark, dreary prison, but he was still anointed and eventually, he was promoted with his anointed self to the palace.

Some of you might think that your dreams are dead, but you are still anointed. Your eyes might be filling up with tears right now, but baby, you are still anointed. The devil thought he had you, but what he did not know was he was pushing you into your purpose, into your destiny, into your deeper anointing. If the devil thought you were a threat before the pit experience, just wait until this is over. If he thought you were anointed before the pit, tell him to pull up a seat and watch what God is about to do in your life.

It is time for you to get up from that pity party and wash the ashes of rejection and disappointment off you and start walking into your destiny, because my next chapter is a new and fresh anointing. The same people who laughed and mocked me and said 'here comes that dreamer again,' you better watch out because that dreamer—like Joseph—just might be your deliverer.

In my last chapter, you saw me in my pit of delays and denials, but delays are not always denial. The Bible says that Joseph's brothers said to each other, 'here comes that dreamer again.' So, to you I say: I double-dog dare you to dream again.

Chapter Five

Dare To Dream Again

And he dreamed yet another dream, and told it his brethren, and said, Behold, I have dreamed a dream more; and, behold, the sun and the moon and the eleven stars made obeisance to me. And he told it to his father, and to his brethren: and his father rebuked him, and said unto him, what is this dream that thou hast dreamed? Shall I and thy mother and thy brethren indeed come to bow down ourselves to thee to the earth? (Genesis 37: 9-10)

The obtaining of one dreams and goals do not happen without great struggle and opposition. As you pursue your dreams, you will lose many relation-ships and the loss of some of these relationships will surprise you. You never thought that they would turn their backs on you. As long as you lived a life of mediocrity, they accepted you. They even pre-tended that they liked you, but when you begin to have a dream for your life, then they are not so comfortable with you and they begin to show their true colors. And they invite you into the woods to kill you.

They want to kill your dreams, but you survive those adverse conditions, dare to dream an even bigger dream. Now it's more than just a multi-colored coat, but it is your future that they want to destroy.

    Joseph was a dreamer and he was favored by his father. What a combination—vision and the father's anointing. But dreaming can be dangerous, and your dreams might land you in a pit. As we stated earlier, as children we were all dreamers. As young girls, we imagined that we were going to live the Cinderella life, and as boys, we all wanted to be Prince Charming. But as we travel these rocky roads, we will face this thing called life and we are confronted with dream killers. We have ID'd these murders as fear, procrastination, low self-esteem, lack of finances, and pure laziness.

We have seen that one of our main dream killers is people. We understand that people who do not have a dream of their own cannot celebrate your dream. That is why it is important that we surround ourselves with likeminded people. There are not many dreamers left because most them have succumbed to the injuries inflicted on them by the dream killers. And the devil is not the only suspect, but he has many accomplices that are found in the church sitting in the pews right next to you. And some even dare to sit in the pulpit. It was not strangers who tried to destroy Joseph, but it was his own flesh and blood.

Dreamers will always face opposition to their dreams. It takes a great deal of courage and faith to dare to dream again—to dare to dream again in the presence of your haters, dream killers, and non-dreamers. Dreamers are not able to keep their dreams to their selves; they are just too excited about what God is about to do in their lives, they do not care what it looks like now. They are not looking at the now, but at the after.

Being confident of this one thing, that he which hath begun a good work in you will perform it until the day of Jesus Christ. (Philippians 1:6)

God has a plan and a purpose for your life, and regardless of the situation or circumstances that you may now find yourself in, your greatest days are ahead of you, not behind you. You are not a finished product; you have not reached your full potential in God. The work that God has begun in you, He will complete. You may be in the middle of one of the fiercest battles in your life; the enemy has made an all-out attack against you. He may have attacked your marriage, family, finances—even your relationship with God. You may be in the middle of a sickness, trial, or setback that with your natural eye you cannot see any way out of it. But your present situation is not your destination. God will bring to pass everything that has been prophesied over your life. God will fulfill everything that He has promised you. Hell doesn't have enough devils and you don't have enough haters to keep God's plan and purpose for your life from being fulfilled.

A setback in life doesn't mean that it is over. Setbacks are positioning for your comeback. There is not a pit deep enough. A fire hot enough. There is not a chain strong enough to hold you back. You were created to be victorious. You were born to be a winner.

You are not an accident or a mistake. Beloved, hell is not fighting you because of who you are now, but hell is fighting your destiny because the enemy understands that your present situation is not your destination.

He wants to keep you from your purpose and becoming what God has already predestined for you to become. When the enemy sees you, he sees your destiny.

Hell is not fighting because of your present situation, but the enemy is fighting your future. If Joseph had never had the promise of his destiny, he would have never had to go from the pit to the palace, to the prison to his destiny. Your future is a hundred times better than your past, so stop being chained to your past. Your past is over. Everything that God has promised you has to come to pass because:

God is not a man, that he should lay, neither the son of man, that he should repent; hath he said it and shall he not do it? Or hath he spoken it, and shall not make it good? (Number 23:19)

Your future is so much better than your past. That's why the enemy wants to keep you in your yesterdays. Have you ever noticed that the devil never talks about your future, he only reminds you of your past? The enemy's greatest fear is your tomorrow. He understands that greater is coming, but if he can only keep you focusing on your past, he can delay your blessings. Satan wants to frustrate your purpose; he wants you to throw in the towel. You must stop looking at what you are going through and start anticipating where you are going to.

Satan doesn't want you to go where God says you can go, and he doesn't want you to have what God says that you can have. You must understand that the attack is against your purpose. Joseph's brothers didn't try to kill him because of who he was then, because he was only a little boy with a dream, but they tried to destroy his destiny. The good news is that it doesn't matter who or what comes against you if God is for you. The devil cannot kill you because if he could, he would have already. Despite everything that you have been through, despite all the hurt, mistakes, and regrets, the enemy couldn't take you out because you are still standing.

When I look back over my own life and all that I have been through, all the hell I have walked through and all that I have gone through to get to the place where I am now. I am a survivor. Others would have lost their mind and others would have given up. But I am a survivor because God has always been on my side. You are about to become what God has said that you would become. You are about to go where God said you would go. You are about to get what God said you can have. Somebody ought to be shouting right now because you are closer to your destiny than you were yesterday. Because you refused to give up, because despite all that you went through, you remained faithful, because you got up every time the devil knocked you down.

God is turning around for you. You are getting ready to dream again. You have sowed in tears, but now you are going to reap with joy. Your haters are going to say God has done great things for you. You are not just coming out of what you've been in, but you are coming out more blessed than you were when you went in. The chapters are ending and the pages are turning. Your situation is changing. Regardless of what you see, your present situation is not your destination, but you are getting ready to step into your purpose and your destiny.

Starting over again is a new beginning. Starting all over again is important at the end of different seasons in our life. But before you can start all over again, it's important that you take a look back, to reflect on your past failures, successes, and mistakes, to look around to see what state you are presently in and to look ahead to your future.

At the end of certain seasons in our life, we realize that it is not working and we need to start over again. The one thing that most people are afraid of is change because oftentimes, change represents the unknown and even if we are not happy with our current situation, it is what we are used to, so we settle for mediocrity rather than change.

We should not allow our past to define our future. When we look back, it is not to stay there, but for reflecting. Some of us cannot move ahead and start over because we find it hard to let go of the past. It's imperative that we let go of the past because it helps you to live your best life now.

You are fearfully and wonderfully made by God. He has put great things in you. Allow your past to be a learning tool to move forward. We gain so much from our past experiences. Don't allow your past disappointments to determine your future life. You have to make a commitment to leave the past behind you. You should only use your past as motivation to push you forward. When you look back, use it only to drive you forward. When you look around you will have to evaluate who you are and what you are doing right now.

- What are your dreams?
- Goals?
- Visions and aspirations?
- What are your gifts and talents?
- Are you a dreamer or a visionary?

Dreamers are satisfied with the status quo and they are afraid to start over again especially after a failed attempt. Every vision starts with a dream, but it moves past just dreaming and it requires action.

Every great dream begins with a dreamer. Always remember, you have within you the strength, the patience, and the passion to reach for the stars to change the world. ~ Harriet Tubman

Do you have a long list of dreams, visions, aspirations, and goals that you have written down in hundreds of notebooks and journals? How many prophets has God sent to speak a word over your life and you still have not begun to walk into your destiny? What are you presently doing to work towards these goals and objectives? Too many of us are living our lives void of chasing after our dreams and visions. Many of us travel life's roads without setting life goals. What is the purpose of God speaking over your life if you are going to continue year after year just writing in your journal?

While we are looking around we can get stuck in our present situations and circumstances, but we need to look ahead to our future. Sometimes our dreams will not happen overnight; at times it will feel like it's been a long time coming and sometimes it seems like the things that we desire, we will never obtain. But we want our dreams to happen right away. If I am going to be real with you, sometimes it will take a long time for our dreams to be manifested.

Let's look at some people who waited on their dreams for years: The children of Israel wandered around in the wilderness for forty years before they reached the promised land. David was anointed king, but went back into the field tending sheep for many years before he was appointed King. It took Joseph thirteen years to go from dreamer, to the pit, to the palace before his dreams came to fruition. These men were just not dreamers, but they were visionaries.

Visionaries take the actions to move their visions from dreams to reality, but dreamers just sit on the dock of the bay wasting time. Visionaries are not stuck in the past or the present, but they set goals for the future; they are passionate about their future. It is always in front of them; they never lose sight of it.

Now that we have looked back at the past and looked around at our present, now it's time to look ahead to the future. It's time for many of us to revamp and start all over again.

What are your dreams, goals and vision? Take out those notebooks and journals and start moving from dreamer to visionary. Do you want to start a business? So what if you started a business before and it failed. It's time to start again. You want to go back to school to get that GED or bachelors or masters degree? So you failed out the last time you went to school, it's time to start again. You want to write a book? The last book you wrote, the publishers rejected it. It's time to write again.

> *Remember not the former things, nor consider the things of old. Behold I am doing a new thing now, it springs forth, do you not perceive it? I will make a way in the wilderness and rivers in the desert. (Isaiah 43:18-19)*

So it's time to dare to dream again. The first thing that you have to do is decide that you are going to do it this time—nothing and no one can stop what God has ordained. Tell other likeminded people that you are ready to dream again, but try to avoid dream killers. But if you do meet the former things that tried to kill you dry, give no place to them, but continue to chase after your dreams. Do not allow them to evade you this time.

Now is the time for you to develop a step by step plan. Write down your dreams and your goals and have a written plan on how you are going to achieve them. Have a timeline and set small attainable goals and give every goal a due date. Write down your action steps—what you will do and how you will do it, what resources you will need and how can you obtain them. During this process, you will begin to evaluate and regulate how you are progressing and if you are headed in the right direction.

There is no better time than today to dare to dream again, so go get your dream back. It is celebration time; you are finally on your way. I dare you to dream again. Look out—here comes the dreamer!

ACKNOWLEDGEMENTS

I would first like to give thanks to my Lord and Savior Jesus Christ through which all blessings flow.

I would like to thank my family: my sisters Gloria, Allison, and Kim, my brothers Samuel, Darren, and Greg. My Mother Willie Mae Millner and my uncle M, C for always seeing the greatness in me and recognizing my potential when I could not see it. And to my daughter Sabria who spent countless hours in the library and never complained - you are my why never give up on your dreams.

To my church family Bishop Williams and Evangelist Billups and the members of The Church Of Jesus Christ Our Lord: thank you for pushing me to my next. In loving memory of Mattie Angus who never let me give up on my dreams.

To Amityville Head Start: continue to think outside the box and never give up on your dreams. To Alicia Marks who always supports me in every endeavor. To my best friends Desiree Sessions, Nydia Paulino, and Gail Williams and Erika Moore - you women are my rock. I love you to life.

To My UNAYO family: thank you from the bottom of my heart in my lowest moments you were there. To my publisher Sharnel Williams: you unlocked the beast in me; you believed in me when I was living among my dream killers. To all my Judas's and haters: thank you for propelling me into my destiny. And lastly, to my readers: thank you for investing in my dream and prayerfully, this will encourage you to dare to dream again.